See What I Mean?

See What I Mean?

Poems by

Charles Rammelkamp

© 2023 Charles Rammelkamp. All rights reserved.
This material may not be reproduced in any form, published,
reprinted, recorded, performed, broadcast,
rewritten or redistributed without
the explicit permission of Charles Rammelkamp.
All such actions are strictly prohibited by law.

Cover art by *Saint Louis Post-Dispatch* political cartoonist,
Daniel Fitzpatrick, *Julian S. Rammelkamp,* 1951
Cover design by Shay Culligan

ISBN: 978-1-63980-447-4

Kelsay Books
502 South 1040 East, A-119
American Fork, Utah 84003
Kelsaybooks.com

This book is for Abby, Anna, and Zoë,
who generally know what I am getting at.

"I don't seem to know what I think until I see what I say."
—Saul Bellow, *Humboldt's Gift*

Acknowledgments

Thank you to the following publications, where versions of these poems previously appeared:

Bindweed: "Turn stored tension into creativity"
Blood and Thunder: "Rashida and the Beast"
Branching Out: Brilliant Flash Fiction Anthology: "Birdwatching"
Cajun Mutt Press: "Andrew Jackson's Parrot," "Nice Rack"
Calliope: "The Houdini Séance"
Chiron Review: "In Her Novel," "The Last Good Country," "Maquiladora Madness," "Recognize This?" "What We Talk About When We Talk About Sex"
Dark Winter Lit: "The Third Person"
Evening Street Review: "Almost as Intimate as Kissing," "Cover Up," "Justice"
Exit 13: "The Diamond Dog," "Translate This"
The Fictional Café: "The Anatomy Museum," "Chess," "Don Samuel," "Little Red Man," "Manchester United," "Roget at the Pneumatic Institute, 1800," "Roget's Strumpet"
The Five Two Crime Poetry: "The Day Sadat Died"
Garfield Lake Review: "Combat!"
Gargoyle: "AuH2O," "Joyeux Noël"
Glimpse: "Flights of Fancy"
Green Hills Literary Lantern: "Public Service Initiative," "The Afterlife"
Home Planet News: "Assassin," "Bomb Scare," "Peter Roget Escapes," "Terrorism," "Would You Like to Come in for a Drink?"
Horror, Sleaze, Trash: "Jimmy Blanchard Waits for the Light to Change," "Tina James Raises Her Voice," "The Sex Nerve"
Iconoclast: "Commencement"
The Lake: "There she is, your ideal"
Literary Cocktail: "Charlie Is My Darling"
London Grip: "Get Out of Jail Free"

Main Street Rag: "Karl van Beethoven Considers Suicide," "The Heiligenstadt Testament"
Meat for Tea: "Anarhy," "Antarctic Discoveries," "The Sex Side of Life"
North of Oxford: "Coronavirus Cooties," "Pandemic"
NYC From the Inside (anthology, Blue Light Press): "Ode to the Orange Bear"
Off Course: "Bambi," "Contact High," "Notes from the Upper East Side," "Pranayama," "The Vending Machine Tango"
Otherwise Engaged: "Invasion," "Like Romeo and Juliet, Only Tragic," "Ode to Coffee"
Panoplyzine: "Rivals"
The Poeming Pigeon: "The Scourge"
Poetry and Covid: "My Big Sister Gets Vaccinated"
Qua: "Free Your Hips," "Slow Gun"
Slipstream: "Haunt"
Song of the San Joaquin: "You Say Tomato, I Say Matato"
Speckled Trout Review: "A Synonym for Surprise"
Valley Voices: "Before He Left the Room," "Escape from Treblinka," "Study Art"
Waterways: "Odobenidae," "Punk Rock Warlord"
The Zodiac Review: "Linger Stink," "Wise Man"

Contents

The Meat at the End of the Fork

Public Service Initiative	15
The Cover Up	17
Peace	19
Justice	20
Anarhy	21
AuH2O	22
My Big Sister Gets Vaccinated	23
I'm Not Throwing Away My Shot	24
Rashida and the Beast	25
Pandemic	26
Punk Rock Warlord	27
Get Out of Jail Free	28
Coronavirus Cooties	30
Terrorism	31
Bomb Scare	32
Ode to the Orange Bear	33
Clear *What* Up?	35
Combat!	37
Invasion	38
The Diamond Dog	39
The Third Person	40
Translate This	41
Haunt	42
Like Romeo and Juliet, Only Tragic	43
Would You Like to Come in for a Drink?	45
What We Talk About When We Talk About Sex	46
Twitterpated	47
Odobenidae	48
Flights of Fancy	49
The Last Good Country	50

Contact High	51
Ode to Coffee	53
You Say Tomato, I Say Matato	54
In Her Novel	55
Charlie Is My Darling	56
Almost as Intimate as Kissing	57
Notes from the Upper East Side	60
Joyeux Noël	61
Nice Rack	63
PTSD	64
The Vending Machine Tango	66
A Synonym for Surprise	68
Facebook Afterlife	69
The Afterlife	70
Study Art	71
Recognize This?	72
Slow Gun	73

And the Rest Is History

Little Red Man	77
Roget at the Pneumatic Institute, 1800	79
Peter Roget Escapes	80
The Anatomy Museum	82
Chess	83
Manchester United	84
Uncle Sam	85
Sir Samuel	86
The Suicide	87
Don Samuel	89
Dylan Thomas's Substitute for Inspiration	91
Roget's Strumpet	93
The Houdini Séance	94

Karl van Beethoven Considers Suicide	98
The Heiligenstadt Testament	99
Königin der Nacht	100
Pranayama	101
Bambi	102
Escape from Treblinka	103
Jimmy Blanchard Waits for the Light to Change	104
Tina James Raises Her Voice	106
Maquiladora Madness	108
Andrew Jackson's Parrot	110
The Day Sadat Died	111
Assassin	113
Before He Left the Room	115
Commencement	117
The Scourge	119
Antarctic Discoveries	120
"Turn stored tension into creativity,"	122
The Sex Nerve	123
Free Your Hips	125
Linger Stink	126
Birdwatching	128
Wise Man	130
There she is, your ideal	132
The Sex Side of Life	134
Rivals	136

The Meat at the End of the Fork

Public Service Initiative

"We're from the Mayor's Office
of Emergency Management," I smiled
at the elderly black lady
cowering behind the front door
of the dilapidated rowhouse
in the rundown urban neighborhood
that I'd just pounded like a warning.
"We're here to see if you need
any smoke detectors or energy efficient
light bulbs, or if you need your blood
pressure taken, or anything."

Volunteer work with the fire department,
health officials, public works and cops.
Yet people had warned me:
wear your Kevlar vest
when you're in *that* neighborhood!

But it seemed *I* was the predator,
the threatening outsider,
not some gang member or hoodlum
come to prey on the weak.

Hesitant, not sure whether to trust
the lime-green vest and ballcap
with something about the city
in white block letters on the visor,
the old woman weighed the alternatives
like blindfolded Justice: free services
or an intrusive government busybody—
there to fine, threaten, or scold?

"We fine," the quavering voice
finally announced.
"We don't need nothin'."

I nodded and left, feeling like a fraud.

The Cover Up

> "Every year it was one of the most stolen books from the Tulsa library system. Every year I would send them a new box."
> —Scott Ellsworth, author of *Death in a Promised Land: The Tulsa Race Riot of 1921*

In the late fifties I was teaching history
at Booker T. Washington High in Tulsa
when I told my students
about the massacre in 1921.

"The whites came over the tracks,
machine guns blazing, wiped out Greenwood,
probably more than three hundred dead."
In fact, I told them, they'd used this building,
Booker T. High, as a hospital for colored folks.

"I don't believe that!" one of my students shouted,
a pool hustler named Don Ross.
"How come don't nobody know
nothing about it, Mr. Williams?"

But I remember. I was sixteen,
fighting next to my father,
trying to save our building, our business,
Williams Confectionery, down the block
from our other business, Dreamland Theater,
corner of Greenwood and Archer.

The whites finally overwhelmed us.
They marched me down Greenwood,
my arms reaching for empty sky.
I watched a white boy running from our house,
a fur coat belonging to my mother
clutched to his chest like the pelt
of some animal he'd just killed.

Next day I showed Don Ross the pictures,
charred corpses and burned-out buildings,
took him to meet other survivors.
How come don't nobody know nothing?
I told Ross: "Because the killers
are still in charge of this town, boy."

Peace

Just before they stormed the barricades,
the Proud Boys gathered near the Peace Memorial,
at the foot of Capitol Hill,
where fifty years earlier
my friends and I planted flags
protesting the Vietnam War.

"A mishmash monument," one scholar called it,
the muse of History on top,
forever reading the words,
"they died that their country might live,"
from the book she holds in her left hand,
while Grief hangs on her left shoulder,
weeping, and Victory gloats beneath them,
baby Mars and Neptune,
like cherubim in a sandbox,
playing with their sword and trident,
at Victory's feet.

And Peace?
Bare-breasted, she stands alone
on the other side of the monument.

The beefy men in MAGA hats,
waving "Stop the Steal" banners,
bellowed like wild beasts
at the very place, a few days later,
photographs of Brian Sicknick,
the Capitol cop killed in the mob attack,
appeared next to flowers and American flags.

Justice

My college friends and I all took heart
when the Supreme Court voted 5-4
in favor of the teenager who wore the jacket
with FUCK THE DRAFT on the back
when he walked through a courthouse corridor
on his way to a courtroom.
Protected by the First and Fourteenth Amendments.
It was 1971. Our student deferments
wouldn't last forever,
but sometimes it felt like the war would.

"One man's vulgarity is another's lyric,"
Justice John Marshall Harlan wrote
in the decision to overturn the ruling.
The kid, Paul Cohen, had been convicted
of disturbing the peace,
sentenced to thirty days in jail.

When the case was remanded for formal dismissal,
Cohen had to return to the court.
"The judge was upset
with the Supreme Court's ruling,"
he recalled years later,
"but I probably angered him more
when I asked for my jacket back."

Anarhy

For E and J

When I saw the word scrawled
into sidewalk outside the art school,
I wondered if the misspelling were deliberate,
the concept made manifest
in the contempt for rules of language,
as well as the defacement of property itself,
the word etched into the gray mortar
with a sharp stick, like a poke in the eye.

Or had the kid (who else?),
in his rush not to get caught,
simply scratched in haste,
missing the c, not realizing his mistake?
Or did he really not know
how to spell the word?

And I remembered the Sex Pistols,
coolest name for a band
until Pussy Riot came along,
with Johnny Rotten and Sid Vicious
and their *fuck-you* attitudes;
the ransom-note typography
on their one and only record album,
a group that imploded almost
before they'd even established themselves:
now *that's* anarchy for you.
Or, anarhy.

AuH2O

"The cocksucker's voting for Goldwater."
I pointed an accusing finger at the bumper sticker
adorning the Dodge Dart's chrome fender.
The one on my parents' Studebaker read:
"All the Way with LBJ."

Heading home after school
that idiot crisp October day,
Howard and I'd passed the car
parked at the curb a block away
from Potawatomi Rapids Junior High.
Only fourteen at the time,
all we really knew about politics
was our parents voted Democrat,
and Republicans were uptight assholes.

It was all we thought
we needed to know:
the elements of politics
reduced to their yin and yang,
their yes and no.
Who were you for? Who against?

"Let's bust his fuckin' headlight,"
Howard dared, and by "we"
he meant me.
Or was I too scared to do it?
This is what we meant by "elemental."

My Big Sister Gets Vaccinated

Juanita refused to get the polio shot.
At sixteen, she claimed she was careful, safe.
I'd gotten mine, but I was eight years younger;
my parents made the decision,
but that didn't stop Juanita
looking at me as if I were some kind of traitor.

"I don't *like* getting needles stuck in my arm!"
she wailed, operatic. She always made
a big production, her life an epic drama.

"But Juanita!" Mom and Dad cried back,
wringing their hands, playing their parts
in our family melodrama.

So what changed her mind?
Just before his historic 1956 performance
on "The Ed Sullivan Show," Elvis Presley
agreed to get jabbed in his arm
in front of the cameras, the photos
influencing teens nationwide.
Suddenly it seemed sexy to her, hip.
Four years later, polio incidence
only a tenth what it had been in 1950.

Now I've just received my second Moderna shot.
A mild fever and aching bones but worth it.
Juanita? Not so lucky. Died in her nursing home
before the vaccines had been developed.

I'm Not Throwing Away My Shot

We pulled into the pharmacy parking lot
across the street from a three-story mural
painted on the side of an apartment building
in this unfamiliar part of town,
George Floyd's baleful eyes looking down at us,
making me think of T.J. Eckleburg,
the billboard in *The Great Gatsby,*
gazing down on the American moral wasteland.

We'd come here for our Moderna vaccinations,
having scored appointments early one morning online,
a sort of macabre competition for shots
a friend likened to *The Hunger Games.*

Inside the drug store,
we went through the sign-in procedure,
displaying ID and insurance information,
then took our place in line
on the molded plastic waiting-area chairs,
spread apart at the required distance.

Only after we'd had our shots
did we realize the other people
in front and behind us
were likewise white senior citizens,
the only Caucasians in this store,
all the other customers and employees African-American;
the means to secure vaccinations
favoring those with computers and internet access.

Driving home under Floyd's soulful stare,
we felt guilty about our white privilege,
but grateful for the immunization.
Or, were we grateful for the immunization, first,
but guilty about our white privilege?

Rashida and the Beast

When the coronavirus spread like oil
from a wounded tanker in the Mediterranean,
through the country and around the world,
I had to move my animals
from the circus in Suez
where we'd been performing
to our desert compound outside Cairo,
eight lions and three tigers,
around six thousand feline pounds,
not easy for a 130-pound woman and her entourage!

But I love my job,
dressed in my leopard-skin body suit,
high black leather boots,
wielding the batons and whips of my profession
like some badass dominatrix on Broadway;
but there's nothing to it, really,
coaxing my babies through rings of fire,
charming them to walk over my body
as I lie spread-eagled in the ring.
Like any man, give them affection
and morsels of donkey meat,
and they'll do anything for you!

Lions and tigers are so much easier
to deal with than the schoolchildren
and their swaddled-up mothers
who come to our shows.
As another famous lion tamer,
Maria Rasputin, once observed
when asked why she did it,
"Why not? I have been in a cage with Bolsheviks."

So now we wait out the Plague,
a more deadly killer than men or wild animals.

Pandemic

"They called it the 'Black Death,'
because of the color of the gangrenous flesh,"
Mister Philby lectured, my mom's colleague
at the school, here to drop off some papers,
though they were all working from home now.

"Bruised-looking, purplish, like an aubergine.
The bacteria came from fleas,
entered the bloodstream,
clotted on the extremities—nose, hands, feet;
the skin like something
you'd see on trick-or-treaters at Halloween."

Although he wore a mask, Philby was loud,
speaking in what Mom called his "classroom voice."
"It also caused swollen lymph glands," he went on,
"in the groin and armpits.
That's how it got its most popular name,
'the bubonic plague.' The abscessed lymph glands
were called buboes; the Greek word means 'groin.'

"But it all comes from the bacteria,
Yersinia pestis by name.
Deadly. Pisa lost seventy percent of its population
when it hit Europe in the fourteenth century."

This was all kind of interesting,
in a *Trivial Pursuit* sort of way,
like questions on *Jeopardy!*
("I'll take 'Tragedy' for $1,000, Alex.")
But my grandma had coronavirus,
strapped to a hospital bed in Des Moines,
and we weren't allowed to see her.
She'd be dead by the weekend.

Punk Rock Warlord

The last time I saw Mark alive
he stood at the pickle stand
in the throng of the farmers market
that brisk September Sunday morning,
wearing his Punk Rock Warlord t-shirt.

The gentlest man I knew,
my every Wednesday evening yoga teacher
at the Yoga Village, leading us
through downward dogs and cat-cows, leaving us
invigorated, restored, hopeful, meditative.

I caught Mark's eye; we waved.
"See you in class!" I called,
Mark fifteen feet ahead of me.

He smiled. "Maybe. Hope so."
I later found out Mark had just been diagnosed
with a rare neurological disease,
Creutzfeldt-Jakob, like Mad Cow,
eating swiftly through the brain.

"Gotta check out the peppers and cucumbers!"
He left with his container of pickles,
wobbling, a little off-balance,
the punk rock warlord weaving his way
through the crowd, soon disappearing from sight.

Get Out of Jail Free

I've never been one
who cared for class reunions.
Never felt much solidarity
with my classmates—what Vonnegut
called a "granfalloon," a group of people
who affect a shared identity or purpose
but whose association is meaningless.
Never been to a college reunion,
much less one for my high school class.

Not that I had bad feelings
about my contemporaries in my hometown,
just that it seemed a lot of bother
to travel hundreds of miles
to chit-chat with people
I hadn't kept in touch with,
spring for a hotel room,
dip into my precious cache of vacation days.

But this year's my fiftieth
at Potawatomi Rapids High, class of 1970,
and I'm retired now, to boot, no excuses.
The planning committee's even sent
a nifty refrigerator magnet
with the school mascot (a muskrat)
leaping out of the frame.
People have sent me letters and emails
pressuring me to attend, warning
rooms at the Potawatomi Rapids Inn were going fast;
I'd better reserve one soon!

And I'd even asked myself:
If not now, when?
Wasn't I curious to see
how Melissa Bakewell had aged, the girl
for whom I'd pined all those years ago?

But then along came COVID-19.
True, the reunion's not until late July,
but really, is this a good idea?

Coronavirus Cooties

"Daddy, Ian said I had cooties,"
Stephanie pouted to her father
about a kid in her first-grade class.

Amused and gratified to hear
the term still in use,
generations later,
her father asked,
"What *are* cooties?"

"They make you *fat*,"
Stephanie answered without hesitation,
disgusted by the fact,
body-type issues infecting
even elementary school children.

Originally World War One soldier slang
for body lice in the trenches,
cooties had mutated over the years,
just like any other virus.

In her dad's day, girls gave boys cooties,
boys gave them back to girls,
like an unacknowledged venereal disease,
polio in the 1950s,
AIDS in the 1980s.
What next, in 2020?

Terrorism

"Didi, come to my desk right now,"
Sandra shrieked, scurrying into
and out of my cubicle
like a mouse darting into a hole.
I followed her to her computer.

"I just got this email
from somebody I don't even know."
On the screen, a scrambled message
like a ransom note, a jumble of letters and punctuation
out of which the random word "Bomb"
stood like a wound in the flesh
of the computer screen's skin,
swarming with alphanumeric characters.

"Don't open it!" she warned,
voice shrill with near-panic,
even though I stood three feet back,
my hands jammed into my pockets.

"Why don't you forward it
to the security desk?" I advised,
even as I recognized the spam
for discount Viagra pills.

Ever since 9/11, years ago,
Sandra'd been suspicious
as a drug-sniffing bloodhound.
Anything threatening made her tail wag
faster than a windshield wiper in a downpour.
Fire drills frightened her;
she closed her eyes in silent prayer.

Bomb Scare

Oh Lord God.
The Subject line in the email
was a garble of characters,
and I didn't recognize the sender's name.
But the word "Bomb" exploded
from the alphabet soup of type
crawling like bugs across my computer screen.

"Didi!" I yelped, rocketing
out of my chair as if I'd been shot,
hurrying down to my co-worker's cube.
Didi works with the emergency response staff,
so I thought of him first.

"Come here to my desk, please."
I tried to sound calm but I could tell
he knew I was freaked by something.
Ever since 9/11 I take all this seriously,
especially working in a government agency.

"Send that to the security desk, Sandra,"
Didi told me, cool as an after-work drink.
He even looked like he was smiling,
as if he found it funny.
I know I shouldn't be so scared,
but when you lose somebody you know
like I did at the Pentagon that day,
you don't get over it so easy.

Ode to the Orange Bear

I'd arranged the poetry reading for October,
but the Orange Bear, where the reading took place,
was on Murray Street, in the financial district,
only blocks from where the World Trade Center towers
had collapsed in fire and rubble only a month before.

We moved the reading up to mid-January.
I took the Metroliner up from Maryland,
my friend Roger meeting me at Penn Station.
We stopped at his office on 53rd Street,
skyscraper windows looking south, downtown.
"I had to look away," Roger confessed. "I couldn't watch."
Of course, we'd all see it over and over again
on television for months to come.

We rode the subway downtown,
emerging like moles into daylight and snow,
a smell of ash and smoke like an invisible shroud,
four months later, the snow
reinforcing the tomb-like serenity.
Tourists milled around the fenced-off crater
where the buildings once stood.

In the Orange Bear, we met Pepper, the host,
who sponsored us to a scotch.
Cigarette smoke hazed the room,
city ordinances be damned, and over
the mahogany bar a cheap painting
of a reclining odalisque hung
like the cover of a pulp fiction novel; a broken-down
pool table in the center of the room
likewise reinforcing the mood.

The first poet, a humanitarian activist,
read poems about tortured children,
raped women, Central American military thugs,
so fitting to the World Trade Center atmosphere.

Then it was my turn.
Already looking forward to my train home,
I stood behind the microphone,
by the wobbly billiards table.

Clear *What* Up?

You signed up for beginning Persian
your senior year
to fulfill a requirement
but also the graceful script,
sinuous as a coil of snakes,
intrigued your imagination;
you wanted to crack the code,
unlock its secrets.

But one day at the gym
you left your flashcards in a locker
and when you returned to retrieve them,
you learned the assistant manager,
a woman so blindingly blond
it made you squint to look at her,
not an ounce of fat apparent on her body—
nor a brain in her head, either—
had given the cards to the police,
suspecting a terrorist plot.

"They were in a box,"
Cathy Larreau pointed out, defensive,
as if this itself suggested danger—
a concealed bomb, hidden stick of dynamite;
not really an apology, more like an accusation.

"You can't be too cautious these days,"
you replied, politely excusing her
but seething from the unnecessary inconvenience,
writing off the loss of the cards.

But as you stood to leave
the assistant manager's office,
a moist cubby near the women's locker room,
jammed with file cabinets and free weights,
reeking of sweat and hairspray,
Cathy warned, "You'd better
clear this up with the police,"
in a voice from Cold War film noir.

Combat!

All of our fathers were World War II vets.
It went with the territory, 1966, ninth grade,
Potawatomi Rapids Junior High.
Tommy Patterson's dad had been on a ship
in the Pacific, fought in Okinawa.
Phil Dulaney's had been in the infantry in Italy.
My father'd spent the war in Panama,
a radar man away from the action overseas.
Even Werner Fischer's papa'd been in the German army,
shrapnel scars along his jaw
where machine gun bullets had grazed him.

But when I learned Bruce Higgins' father,
my high school Civics teacher,
had been in the Normandy invasion,
I raised my hand in class one day
to ask him if he'd killed any Nazis,
a smirk on my face, a huge fan of *Combat!*,
the World War II drama that ran for five years on ABC.

A short, slope-shouldered man in a jacket and tie,
gray hair cut close to his skull,
it felt like I was giving him a chance to brag,
but Mr. Higgins did not crack a smile,
as I'd expected him to, warm to the subject
of his heroic, patriotic feats.

"There's nothing to be proud of," he replied,
his voice cave-hollow, face drawn and ashen.
"We just did what we had to do."

My face burned.
I saw myself through his eyes,
the callow youth that I was.

Invasion

"Lud!" my uncle called from the bathroom.
Frank had just scuttled out of his chair
to the bedroom and beyond,
a wet sound accompanying him
like a witch's familiar,
a messenger, a spy.

Ludmilla, the Russian wife he'd met in the war,
when he'd been stationed in Germany,
exotic to all of us Midwestern relatives,
even forty years later,
in the depths of the Reagan Eighties,
at the Minnesota lakeside cottage
where the family gathered every summer:
somehow she'd managed to be
both peasant and aristocrat,
Frank's family, including his brother Dave, my dad,
totally in awe. Me too:
Zsa Zsa Gabor, my private nickname.

It was a familiar scene, it seemed,
Ludmilla attending to her husband's needs,
urgent, impossible to ignore,
as age assaulted their bodies.

What brings back this memory now?
Hint: it's not Putin's invasion of Ukraine.

The Diamond Dog

> "This ain't rock and roll, this is genocide."
> —David Bowie, "Diamond Dogs"

Our private name for Doctor Jacob Diamond,
our primary care doctor,
may not have been very original,
but Marci and I were always fans—
our first date had been a Bowie concert
at Boston Garden back in the Seventies.
Though not really serious,
we'd even talked about naming our first-born Ziggy,
but then we had a daughter.

Diamond hadn't actually boasted
about his grandparents' immigration from Ukraine,
but you could hear the pride in his voice
when he took your blood pressure
or applied the stethoscope to your chest,
the familiar chit-chat, doctor to patient.

He'd sold the practice to the university,
or so we understood,
moved to Boca Raton.
Now we read his name in the newspaper,
a volunteer in Mariupol, alongside the soldiers
at the Azovstal steelworks
(he *had* to be in his sixties, didn't he?),
offering medical assistance to the resistance fighters.

The Third Person

While at the day care lady's
picking up my daughter after work,
one of the moms, Kathy,
is telling us about an accident
that just happened on Monroe,
a narrow, two-way residential street,
cars parked along the curb
tight as bricks in a wall.

First, a football rolled into the street,
then a boy darted out like a squirrel
between two cars.
The driver of the van
may have been speeding
slightly over the posted limit,
but no way he could have stopped.

Tommy's father comes in
in the middle of the story.
"That happened to George," he mutters,
as if in a trance,
his eyes glassy, masking
a terror so profound
we suddenly can't breathe.

"George was driving up Keswick Road
when the kid ran into the street
chasing a frisbee.
George couldn't stop in time."

What really catches our breath
is the way George speaks
in the third person.

Translate This

When the angry fat man,
jowls dripping down his face
like melting slabs of butter,
blocking the toothpaste aisle
in the pharmacy, sneered,
Why don't you speak English?
to the Palestinian woman,
her hair covered in a bright khimar,
speaking into her cellphone,
his pants, like his jowls,
sliding down his hips,
revealing the shy smile
of a plumber's butt crack,

Asf ya 'umi, she whispered
into the cellphone,
and to the man standing in her way,
Excuse me, may I help you?

Flustered, he stalked away,
pulling up the back of his trousers,
as if this was where his shame lay.

Haunt

"If you don't believe in God,
you can't believe in ghosts,"
Rusty announced, his logic impeccable,
if you thought of God and angels
as the same kind of incorporeal spirits
as ghosts, holy or not.

But Jimmy didn't want to hear it.
Believing in ghosts was subversive,
even if he didn't know that word.
Believing in God was being a sheep,
accepting the electrified fence
of fairy tale punishments.

Jimmy thought more in terms
of "getting into trouble,"
shorthand for sticking it to the Man:
God was the ultimate Man.

Besides, ghosts were cool,
the restless spirits of the dead
coming back to make trouble,
and he half-believed the stories
about Mrs. Graves' dead husband Jim
haunting her after she'd taken
another man home, just weeks
after Jim had died.

Like Romeo and Juliet, Only Tragic

When I read about the girl who tortured
her boyfriend with text messages,
badgering him to kill himself,
he an emotionally fragile teenager;
how he finally leapt from a car garage,
three stories, head first, to instant death;
how authorities recovered her text messages,
romanticizing suicide as the ultimate
sign of love, devotion, *soulmates;*
how prosecutors described the case
as a form of "domestic violence,"
charging the girl with manslaughter—
telling the boy over and over
the world would be better off without him,

I remembered Harlow Jones from high school,
a shy kid in love with Becky Farber,
a popular girl on the cheerleading squad.
Harlow asked Becky out on a date.
They went to a movie together,
but soon after Becky started seeing Brad Horvath.
Depressed, Harlow shut himself up in his truck,
turned on the ignition, died in the garage.

I graduated the next year,
and when my parents died several years later,
I never returned to Potawatomi Rapids
until my fiftieth high school reunion,
where I learned Becky'd married Brad,
but the marriage ended within a year.
She became known as the town whore,
hanging out in bars, going home
with a different guy every weekend,

until a cancer death just two years previous,
found alone in her bedroom after three days.

I wondered if Becky'd felt responsible for Harlow,
if her life took that dive as a result—
not karma, certainly not manslaughter,
but did she feel responsible somehow?

Would You Like to Come in for a Drink?

Ingrid Bergman (Anna) asks Cary Grant (Philip)
at the door to her London digs
in the 1958 film, *Indiscreet,*
after a convivial evening of conversation and wine.
It's a pivotal moment; Philip says yes.

This seems like a memory to me,
but I can't quite pinpoint it.

Would you like to come in for a cup of coffee?
Would you like to come in for a beer?
Would you like to come in?

Cross the threshold;
the vampire invited in;
no stopping him now.

Step over the doorstep.
I want to know you better.

Was I in college?
When I worked at the university?
When I had that job downtown?

Did it really happen to me?
Or was it something I read in a novel?
A movie I saw? A TV show?
Something a friend told me?

Had I assumed I'd been invited in
for different reasons than she really had?

Does this mean what I think it does?

What We Talk About
When We Talk About Sex

In the spam folder, an email
from something called Purple Rhino.
Risk Free Trial. Subject Line:
Have the Kind of Sex Your Friends Talk About.

What kind of sex does Purple Rhino imagine
my friends talk about?
I can only imagine what Purple Rhino imagines
my friends say about their sex lives.
They sure don't say anything to me about it,
for which I'm basically grateful.

"Last night my wife and I . . ."
"My husband loves it when I . . ."
Or maybe, "The neighbors came by the other night,
one thing led to another and before long
there we were, all six of us . . ."

I *know* Purple Rhino doesn't imagine
anybody mentions, say, prostate surgery
that's left him impotent, wearing a diaper,
peeing in his pants.

Or maybe that's just the audience
Purple Rhino is trying to reach.

Twitterpated

If there were witnesses—
and Abby and I are certainly that—
the mallard could be reported for rape.
Those are not consenting adults.

We watch them in the pond,
the modest, brown-mottled hen
fleeing for her life,
the wings flapping frantically
as she skims across the water,
the bright green mallard in hot pursuit.

She shrugs him off, but he persists.
Finally, in what looks like
an attempted drowning
(He held her under the water, officer;
I'm telling you, she couldn't breathe!),
the drake mounts the hen,
her head submerged.
What a brute!

Odobenidae

We stood in the aquarium at the zoo,
humid as an indoor swimming pool,
looking at the walrus, those long tusks,
propped up on its fins as if in a yoga pose.

"Walruses originally lived in the tropics,"
Suzanne said. She knew all about animals,
had a couple of cats, a dog, a parakeet.
"They followed their food sources north,
wound up in the North Pacific and North Atlantic."

I grunted in acknowledgment, marveling
at those incredible tusks;
no wonder the poachers went after them,
the poor things nearly extinct
before governments banned commercial hunting.
They'd developed the ivory tusks over generations
to protect themselves from polar bears,
Suzanne had mentioned.

"They're like mythological creatures," she gushed,
her admiration making her all the more fetching,
eyes a-glitter like jewels.
"Separated by almost twenty million years
from their closest relative, last remaining species
in their family—a name from a Greek word
meaning 'those who walk with their teeth.'"

"I need to make a dentist appointment," I murmured,
remembering the reminder that came in the morning mail.
Suzanne thought this a witty remark,
squeezed my arm. "Come on," she said,
"I need to get back home to walk Jenny."
Suzanne was one of a kind.

Flights of Fancy

Oddly, when the young woman's head
accidentally falls on my shoulder,
as she loses consciousness
in the seat beside mine,
I remember the kid in college in the sauna,
boasting about having sex with the stewardess.
(They were still called that then,
"flight attendant" not yet a job description.)

It was back when they still served hot meals,
even on domestic flights.
The boy, a muscular football player,
bragged how the girl in the airline uniform
brushed his leg when she put the TV dinner
onto his fold-out tray,
rolled her eyes to the cabin in back.

"We did it standing up," he chortled,
"banging against the wall,
her pantyhose dangling from her ankle."

The rest of us on the sauna bench
either grunted in acknowledgment
or just nodded off in the dry heat.
Maybe he hadn't even spoken.
I wondered if he were making it all up.

Just then the woman wakes up,
apologizes for slumping on my shoulder.
"You remind me of my grandfather," she blushes,
a woman about half my age.
I don't tell her what she reminded me of.

The Last Good Country

At the bookstore across the road from Horton Bay,
the proprietor seemed anxious to sell
Hemingway memorabilia to us—
Nick Adams ballcaps at twenty-five bucks a pop,
T-shirts, postcards, aprons, books.
Although a designated historic site,
there wasn't a lot of traffic here
in Boyne City, on Charlevoix Road—
a little off the beaten path from Petoskey.
She seemed a little desperate.

Even for diehard Hemingway buffs,
how could you compete with Cuba, Key West,
Paris and Pamplona?
Besides, Hem never returned
to northern Michigan after 1922,
even if he set so many stories here.

"No thanks, I already own a copy,"
I politely waved her away
when she offered to sell me
a copy of *The Torrents of Spring,*
but I did buy a handful of postcards
and a bookmark for a friend,
a laminated Calvin and Hobbes cartoon strip
about the right way, the wrong way, the Hemingway:
three and half dollars.

Getting back into our car,
I took a last look out into the bay,
fixing it in memory like a postcard.

Contact High

You know how on a humid day
when you step out of an airconditioned building
it's like being gobsmacked by a steaming towel?
It was like that when the college kid
opened the front door,
after we'd already given up,
headed back down the steps,
Abby and I going door to door
registering voters, having been certified
by the State Board of Elections.

The smell of marijuana almost made me choke,
but Abby didn't seem to notice.
"Oh, hey!" the bearded young man said,
surprised to find us there,
reaching into his mailbox.

"Hi! We're here to register voters," Abby announced,
"only eight weeks to the election."
She started to spell out the dismal voter turnout
in our state, part of the script,
but the kid seemed enthusiastic to register,
and we handed him a form and a ballpoint pen.

"You looked kind of surprised when you saw us,"
I noted. "Did you hear the doorbell?"

"Yeah, but I was down in the basement.
I was just coming up to check the mail."

"It's never good news anyway,
when somebody knocks on your door,"
I joked, knowing how annoying we might be.

"I know, right?" he agreed
with the absent-minded honesty of the stoned,
handing back the completed form.
"But thanks for doing this."

When we walked away,
I wasn't sure if my elation came
from registering my first voter
or the contact high from the pot.

Ode to Coffee

We stop at a state-run rest area
heading south on the highway at 90 mph
as if plunging down one of those water slides
at a mega-amusement park,
a stark brick building like a bunker
with a men's and a women's restroom
and a windowless room with cinder block walls
full of road maps and vending machines.

"Gourmet Coffee" one of the machines proclaims,
a shining tower that looks like an idol
to be bowed down to and worshipped.
How that word "gourmet" underscores
the suspect nature of the brew—
hot chocolate, vanilla-flavored java,
decaf and regular,
a buck and a half for a cardboard cup
that will burn your hands to hold.

I decide to skip it, much as I'd like the caffeine,
hold out for a Starbucks or Dunkin' Donuts
somewhere down the road.

Back behind the wheel,
I see a banner on the bumper of the car ahead,
certain it says "Storm Trooper,"
but when I pass it, I see
it really says "Student Driver."

God, I could use a cup of coffee right now.

You Say Tomato, I Say Matato

The beautiful thing about being a grandfather?
You get to choose what you want to be called.
Some go for the traditional Grandpa or Zayde or Opa,
but when Katie was born, I wanted to be called Pops.

The trouble was she had a hard time
getting her mouth and tongue to pronounce it.
It always came out "Posh."

"Adorable!" my wife exclaimed. "And so fitting!"

Not really. I do wear a necktie every day,
even though I've been retired fifteen years,
but in any case, my daughter and her husband
seemed to like it, too.
Now everyone refers to me as Posh.

But it's Katie's pronunciation of tomato
that really sparked my imagination.
She called it a matato,
reversing the m and the t.
Now I can't call that fruit—
or vegetable—anything else.

In Her Novel

"I should put that in my novel," Carolyn would say, or, "I'm putting that in my novel." It was always something grim—her father cheating on her mother, her own ex's alcoholism, an encounter with a teacher in her daughter's elementary school over some behavioral issue. She said it almost as a note to herself, a reminder; sort of a way to settle the score.

I'd never seen this novel, but I had no doubt Carolyn really was working on it. Sometimes she'd make a reference to the main character, who of course was autobiographical even though she spoke of Kara as an almost mythological hero. The novel seemed to be as much therapy as entertainment. Carolyn claimed to have written hundreds of pages already, incidents and dialogue with no real plot structure, though she was always figuring it out, how the story would ultimately shape up. "And it's funny," she assured me, confident about this. "It's going to be *really* funny, laugh-out-loud funny." I didn't doubt this, either, because Carolyn had a very sharp wit.

It was after we broke up that I started to have nagging doubts about appearing in her novel myself. But she wouldn't do this to me, would she? I was never like her ex, her father, her brother, her shitty boss, was I?

Yet I still wake up in a sweat from dreams too painful to contemplate. I only hope that novel never gets published.

Charlie Is My Darling

Watching Ellie look through the old photo album, Duncan remembered the Robert Burns poem, "Charlie Is My Darling."

He set his Jenny on his knee,
All in his Highland dress,
For brawlie weel he kend the way
To please a bonnie lass

"Do you ever think of that guy?" He stabbed a finger at the old boyfriend standing next to her in the college graduation picture, two beaming faces.

"Gary? Not really. He joined the military, fought in Desert Storm, Kuwait. Then I lost touch. He might have gotten married? Probably. We all do."

Duncan knew all of this was true, commonplace. He didn't really feel jealous, but with a pang of something that felt like regret he remembered Betsy O'Neal from his own college days, how he'd had a major crush on her, but they'd just never connected, even though he *knew* the attraction was mutual.

Sometimes when he couldn't sleep Duncan would fantasize being twenty years old all over again, only this time he'd "kend the way to please a bonnie lass."

"Oh, now I remember! He went to work for Northrup Grumman or Lockheed Martin or some two-name defense contractor. Memory Lane, eh?"

Almost as Intimate as Kissing

"Jerome!"

We reach in for the handshake, but then we realize the situation, both of us behind shopping carts at the early morning people-over-sixty grocery hour—like the early-bird dinner the retired Floridians eat, only in reverse—face masks obscuring our mugs, thin disposable gloves covering our hands, like a second layer of skin.

For a couple of weeks, before the six-foot social-distancing rule took effect, the elbow-bump had been trending, and I'd come to like it, as if it were a move on the basketball court, a fake, a fade, a wide-open J.

Jerome and I had had a regular Sunday morning game of one-on-one on the basketball court at the gym, first to score eleven, for close to a decade, until the day my ACL snapped like banjo strings, and I collapsed to the floor, unable to stand on my right leg, wobbly and unstable as a string of al dente spaghetti. Jerome had driven me over to the emergency room and called my wife.

Once I'd healed—I was deep in my fifties by then—we never played another game. But when I took up swimming laps in the pool, before long Jerome, too, joined the little band of early-morning before-work swimmers. We continued to talk basketball up in the locker room, sweating together in the sauna, shaving at the wash basins, showering in adjacent stalls, sitting on the bench in front of the lockers, getting dressed. Kobe, Lebron, the Lakers, the Celtics, Golden State.

Even after we both retired—me from Sales, Jerome from the Law—we continued to show up at the gym before dawn, join the group of swimmers, swap stories in the locker room, then go our separate ways.

Now it had been a couple of months since the gym had closed; governor's orders.

"How's it going?"

I shrug. Such a simple question, but oh, what a complicated answer! So much had happened the past few months. On top of the pandemic, the George Floyd murder had recently happened. My wife and I had social-distance protested at a local rally, standing silent for eight minutes and forty-six seconds, the length of time the police officer had knelt on Floyd's neck. Jerome and I talked politics, too, but this chance meeting in the grocery was more personal than that. The question was more elemental. *How is it going?*

"I was just thinking: I'd be on my annual Chicago-Minneapolis swing about now, if I were still working, talking to clients." Somehow the response didn't seem adequate.

"Tell me about it. The courts are closed to the public. Only essential staff, only emergency matters. Glad I got out when I did."

We share a grim laugh. Gallows humor.

"How's the family?" Jerome's father, long dead now, was African-American, his mother, still alive in her mid-nineties, Italian-American. Jerome married a Scandinavian blonde named Elsa. They have a couple of daughters whom I've never seen; they have their own families out in Oregon or California or someplace. Jerome and I never actually socialized outside of the gym, though once, many years ago, we did have a beer together after a basketball game.

He shrugs. Another complicated simple question. "Yours?"

I shrug, too. My son's career Army, stationed overseas in Frankfurt. He tested positive for COVID like so many of his men, and self-quarantined away from his wife and children for a couple of weeks, but he was never seriously ill.

"Good to see you," I say, almost apologetic because it really is great to see Jerome, even if I can't express it. This is the *friendship* I've found so absent from my life these past months. This is what all that isolation makes you hungry for. My glasses have fogged up with the conversation, my breath clouding the lenses up from under the mask. We push away in opposite directions in the breakfast cereal aisle. "I understand the NBA's talking about having a short season and playoffs, under strict conditions. Too bad it had to happen this way, you know? I thought this might be Milwaukee's year."

"Yeah, or maybe the Lakers'."

There's so much left unsaid, but we're blocking the aisles. I can see the same yearning that I feel for something *normal* in Jerome's eyes. But people are waiting for us to get out of the way, so we move on, resisting the impulse to fist-bump—or even shoulder-pat.

Notes from the Upper East Side

Me? I've been isolating for years.
It's what writers do, right?
This quarantine business is no hardship.
If I don't have to go to a baby shower,
I don't have to buy a pastel skirt suit.

Limiting social contact is easy for me,
but I *have* turned to Instagram
to connect with old friends
I haven't seen since the pandemic.

Last month I came across a photo on Instagram,
an old boyfriend from 1992!
My God, I thought,
what's Julian doing at the Insurrection?

Mystified? You could say that.
Why, we used to have martinis at Bemelmans.

Joyeux Noël

Her eyes alight with mischief,
as if laughing at some private joke,
Miss Brooks stood at our door
that cold December morning
offering a French grammar textbook
to my mother, who'd answered the doorbell.

"Please give this to David," she smiled,
turning back to her car.
"I won't need it until
the new semester begins at the high school."

My brother, home from college
for the Christmas holidays,
had gone out with his buddies
the night before, stumbling in drunk
well past midnight, my father cautioning
my angry mother that David
just needed to blow off some steam
after his grueling freshman semester.

When he saw Miss Brooks' car
at the curb, David had darted up the stairs
like a frightened cat, slamming himself
into his room, cowered behind the closed door.

Miss Brooks was the hottie French teacher
rumored to buy beer
for the boys on the football team,
whispered to do so much more for them.

"I didn't know you were taking French,"
my mother's voice colder
than the Michigan winter outside,
handing him the copy of *Aujourd'hui*.

"I'm thinking about auditing a class
in the spring," David mumbled,
never letting on he and his friends
had banged on their teacher's door
late the night before, thinking
they were in for a different kind of lesson.

Nice Rack

When Melanie posted a selfie
on her Facebook page,
wearing a tight sweater,
her volupté on display,
she wasn't sure how to react
to the comment, "Nice rack,"
left by a man she didn't actually know.

Going through a divorce,
still in her forties,
she was glad for the compliment
on her appearance,
but the comment was crude;
she felt like an object.

Only, wasn't that what Facebook
was all about? Indeed,
what Zuckerberg and his pals at Harvard
originally created Facebook for?
Hadn't she been showing off,
displaying her assets to her own advantage?

In the end, Melanie unfriended the man.
Even though his salacious comment
had gratified her vanity,
she just didn't need this guy in her life.

PTSD

I remember seeing her at the synagogue,
bandages and bruises on her arms, legs, face;
purple welts, swathed in gauze like a mummy,
her right forearm in a sling,
dark and swollen as an aubergine.

Someone had broken into Isabel's apartment,
beat her up when she walked in on the robbery,
a single woman in her 70's.
That kind of thing can leave a person
skittish as a kitten,
jumping at every banged cupboard.

Maybe that was why Isabel started telling
stories about the rabbi.
I'd been there that day
when she stood at the bima after the haftarah blessing,
meandering aimlessly as she spoke about the nephew
who'd just read the Hebrew scripture,
going on and on about Ira's parents, his tutor,
her relationship with them all, her gratitude,
the congregation growing restless,
murmuring like bees as the minutes crept by,
until the rabbi gently suggested she wrap it up.

The next week, at Kiddush,
sipping a cup of Manischewitz,
Isabel described the rabbi's "attack" to me,
how he had shouted at her, bullied her,
insulted and humiliated her in front of everybody,
and, to top it all off, made a pass at her,
a lewd sexual gesture she only hinted at.

I chose not to correct her—
Shulman *had* tried to be diplomatic—
but I changed the subject instead,
afraid to be drawn into her fantasy world.

Only, to how many people
has she told this same story?
The rabbi himself seems to flinch,
as if deflecting a blow,
at the mention of Isabel's name.

The Vending Machine Tango

When the daily trivia fact dropped
into my email inbox
like a Snickers bar rattling onto the plate,
and I read that vending machines kill
thirteen people every year,

I remembered the night shift breakroom
at the record factory when I was in college,
wiped out from six non-stop hours
putting stacks of lps into sleeves,
the sleeves into boxes, the boxes onto pallets;
the heat, the stuffy air, the tedium.

I plunked my coins into the slot,
selecting the letter-number combination
for the package of Fritos,
only to watch it get stuck in the coils
like a fly trapped in a web
behind the aquarium window,
as if the snack machine were flipping
me the bird.

Enraged with the sense of injustice
only an exhausted factory worker can feel,
I bear-hugged the machine
as if grabbing a fat girl at a dance,
the two of us tangoing across the linoleum,
under the fluorescent lights,
shaking it to loosen the corn chips.

The mammoth lost balance,
toppled over onto me,
the back of my head smacking the floor.

"Jesus Christ!" my co-workers yelled,
pulling the fat lady off of me.
I'd get a reprimand from management
for losing my temper, damaging property,
but at least I got the damn Fritos!

A Synonym for Surprise

On the radio this morning
a little interlude interrupts the litany
of imminent disaster and "breaking news":
the world's toughest tongue-twister,
as certified by Guinness—
the sixth sick sheik's sixth sheep's sick.

I remember she sells seashells by the seashore;
Peter Piper picked a peck of pickled peppers;
how much wood would a woodchuck chuck,
and all the rest.

But the twistiest I've heard,
the one that didn't necessarily improve
pronunciation and fluency
but did bring to mind the detours,
sharp curves and abrupt stops looming ahead,
is when my wife
sat at the hospital registration desk
(me there as her emotional support animal)
telling the lady with the clipboard,
Rammelkamp for a mammogram.

Facebook Afterlife

I wished Abernathy a belated happy birthday,
having noticed on my Facebook page
his birthday occurred two days before.

Only then did I remember
Abernathy'd died six months earlier—
he'd "become late," as they say
in the Botswana lady detectives novels;
he'd "passed," as my friend Lewis puts it.

I'd read somewhere
that not so long from now
more than half of the Facebook accounts
will be owned by dead people.
Unclear who notifies whom
to remove the page, the contact.

This has happened to me before—
a birthday wish to a young woman friend
who'd died from ovarian cancer in her thirties,
another to a poet friend who'd taken his life.

It makes me ponder about the Afterlife—
Heaven or Hades or Nirvana,
Paradise, Valhalla, the Gardens of Delight,
joining the ancestors in The Dreaming,
absorbed into Nature,
one with the trees, the ocean, the sky.
Or Facebook.

The Afterlife

For years after Grover died,
the cash register at the supermarket
spat coupons, like lottery tickets,
for Fancy Feast, Friskies, 9Lives
and other cat food brands,
along with my receipt,
having tracked my purchases
through my "bonus card,"
the ID that saves me money
on various store items.
("You've saved $256.00 this year!"
the cash register tape declares,
triumphant as a Final Four basketball team.)

It was kind of gratifying, though,
to be identified as a cat owner,
a member of the club,
Grover still part of my life,
as if purring away in kitty heaven.

It reminded me of the email
I received from my mother
three months after she died,
somebody having highjacked her account,
spammed her address book
with a promo for a vitamin supplement
meant to prolong our lives.
What a shock to see Mom's name
highlighted in an unopened email,
as if all I had to do
was press REPLY
to talk to her again.

Study Art

The oval frames with the command,
paintbrushes sticking out like quills,
and a rectangular caption completing the thought:
For FUN or FAME;

and on another wall, a similar piece
but with the caption:
For PRIDE or POWER;

and in another room:
For PRESTIGE or SPITE.

And we wander along
through the rest of the exhibit
called Indecent Exposure,
feeling as if
we are in on the joke.

Recognize This?

I was disappointed when I learned
the little plastic disk
we used to snap into singles
to play on the record player
was called a "45 RPM adapter."
It deserved a word of its own.

But the homeless guy
with the Walt Whitman beard
and Charlie Manson eyes
who sleeps under the bridge—
a real fairy tale troll—
knew what it was
when he saw the emblem
on my T-shirt.

He mumbled some private joke,
so private only he understood,
but all at once I recognized him
as a mensch, a well-meaning guy,
if admittedly a little weird.

We bumped fists,
and I continued on my way.

Slow Gun

> "You don't take nothin' with you but your soul."
> —"The Ballad of John and Yoko"

We've all experienced the situation
where you're walking down the street
and somebody comments
on the t-shirt you're wearing.
The comment's usually baffling, a non sequitur,
but then it comes to you;
you look down at your shirt.

"I prefer vinyl to CDs, too," a guy says to me
as we pass one another on the street.
I smile at him like one of us is the village idiot.
Then I realize he's talking about the 45-adapter image
on my t-shirt, the little doohickey you used
to stick into the record single so you could play it
on the long-player turntable.

So I'm walking home with a pizza
for Friday night dinner,
and a guy passes me wearing a t-shirt that says,
"I ♥ Eternal Damnation".
I smile and say to him, "Me too!"
He looks at me like I'm from outer space,
but the woman he's walking with laughs.

And the Rest Is History

Little Red Man

My minister father composed sermons.
My uncle praised their "taste and elegance":
a word man long before me.
Son of a Geneva clockmaker,
mon père, Jean Roget—
"little red man," from the French *rouge*—
immigrated to London at 24
to become pastor at Le Quarré,
the French Protestant church in Soho.

Papa preached in the little Huguenot church
on Little Dean Street,
a few blocks north of St. James's,
the colossus near Piccadilly Circus,
Christopher Wren's largest church—
where I was christened in 1779.

Papa'd married Catherine Romilly a year before,
in St. Marleybone Church,
welcomed into their family without reservation.
My uncle, Samuel, rhapsodized about our happiness,
"as complete as is ever the portion of human beings,"
but only months after my birth,
Papa was "seized with an inflammation of the lungs,"
as my uncle described it,
"attended with a violent spitting of blood."

Papa and Mama left for Switzerland,
hoping a rest cure might save him,
leaving me with my grandparents in London.
I wouldn't see my parents for two years,
when Uncle Samuel took me to Switzerland.
Papa'd resigned from Le Quarré,
knowing he'd never return to England.

He died in the spring of 1783,
soon after my sister Annette's birth.
I'd just turned four that January.

Roget at the Pneumatic Institute, 1800

Coleridge couldn't get enough of it—
a kid in a candy store:
"The first time I felt a pleasurable sensation of warmth
all over my whole frame," he confessed,
"the fourth time more unmingled pleasure
than I had ever before experienced."
Humphry Davy loved nitrous oxide, too;
it gave him a sensation bordering on ecstasy, he claimed.
Robert Southey, the poet, wrote in praise
of the potential benefits of pneumatic medicines.

But Peter Roget? He agreed to take it
because he was working for Davy
at Bristol's Pneumatic Institute, Thomas Beddoes' baby;
Beddoes had written a book
on the treatment of Pulmonary Consumption.
They'd hoped to use nitrous oxide
for their tubercular patients.
The disease had taken Peter's father Jean,
when he was still practically an infant,
so he'd been eager to help.

But Peter didn't enjoy it; he felt queasy,
lost control of his rational faculties.
Sucking down several quarts of the gas,
he just felt dizzy, the room spinning.

The Institute closed after a couple of years.
Nitrous had some fleeting effects
on the healthy volunteers,
but it did nothing for the patients with tuberculosis.

In the end, it would be the mid-century anesthesiologists
who'd discover nitrous oxide's value
for numbing pain during surgical procedures.

Peter Roget Escapes

I'd just graduated from medical school,
didn't know what to do next—
performed odd jobs, took extra courses,
even volunteered as a test subject
for a nitrous oxide trial
at the Pneumatic Institution in Clifton.

Seeing me despondent, flailing about,
my uncle got me a position as a chaperone
for the two teenaged sons of John Philips,
a wealthy cotton mill owner in Manchester,
a year-long trip to the continent,
to learn French before joining the business.

Brits now flocked to France
after eight long years of war,
the peace treaty signed in Amiens closing it out.
Off we went in February of 1802,
only weeks after I'd turned twenty-three.

The boys and I had a great time in Paris,
even saw Napoleon at the Tuileries Palace,
then on to Geneva, where our luck ran out.

Imperial Napoleon had marched
on Italy, Holland, Switzerland,
so King George III declared war on France
just a year after the armistice.
The French retaliated, British citizens
declared prisoners of war,
to be transported to Verdun.

I sent Burton and Nathaniel to
their father's associates in Neuchâtel,
tried establishing Swiss citizenship,
since my late father hailed from Geneva,
but in the end, the boys and I sneaked off,
through obscure villages,
disguising ourselves in shabby clothes,
only speaking French,
bribed a French guard with a bottle of wine,
crossed the Rhine into Germany.

Free at last! It was like waking from a nightmare!
We'd escaped—absconded, evaded, avoided,
extricated ourselves, fled, scrammed, vanished,
saved our necks, slipped away, broke out:
we'd taken French-leave!

The Anatomy Museum

I'd just turned twenty-seven
when I began my lecture series on physiology
for the university students in Manchester,
where I'd already been seeing patients
at the Infirmary, for over a year.

The lectures took place at the anatomy museum
Dr. White, the founder of the Manchester Infirmary,
maintained in his house on King Street
where my modest apartment was, too.

What an eminence, Charles White!
He'd saved so many new mothers dying
from puerperal fever by developing
measures for sanitizing maternity wards.

Skeletons and "specimens" festooned the room
like odd decorations, including a jar labeled
"African Penis: Multo Firmior et Durior."

But the freakiest exhibit in White's museum?
The grandfather clock at the back.
A wealthy female patient left him 25,000 pounds
in her will, with a single stipulation:
once a year he had to view her embalmed body.
White stuffed the mummy inside the clock,
and yes, once a year, accompanied by colleagues,
he peeked inside.

Nervous, averting my eyes from the clock,
I began my first lecture.
"The study of anatomy and physiology is highly interesting . . ."

(Absorbing, engrossing, fascinating, riveting,
gripping, compelling, engaging, though-provoking . . .)

Chess

A polymath—or *nerd,* the term coined
a century and half later—
Roget researched articles for *Encyclopedia Britannica,*
perfected the slide rule to calculate
roots and powers of numbers—
no mere abacus, the forerunner of the calculator
that rendered it obsolete in the 1970's,
more than a hundred years after he died.
Is it any surprise he loved chess, too?

For Roget, chess wasn't simply a pastime, a game,
but something like an academic discipline.
He'd even publish a paper titled,
"Description of Moving the Knight
over Every Square of a Chessboard
Without Going Twice over Any One."

He even invented a pocket chess set,
the Economic Chessboard, one of the first,
marketed in 1846 by De La Rue.

Wonk, geek, trainspotter, obsessive.

Manchester United

My aunt and uncle rescued me from Manchester.
Not that it was *that* bad—
filthy, true, the industrial waste
of "Cottonopolis" overwhelming—
smoke and ashes from the factory chimneys
blanketing the city in soot,
the dyehouses turning the Mersey and Irwell black,
Watts' steam engines polluting the air.

But my colleague Dr. John Ferriar and I
worked to put Manchester on the map,
a center for the upcoming field of public health.
We treated the sick; we saved lives.

Still, four years after I got there,
Uncle Samuel's dear wife Anne wrote me,
"Your uncle and I have frequently
been lamenting that your time and talent
should be so thrown away in *Manchester.*"

London snobs? Well, they had a point.
I'd come to Manchester for the opportunity
to be a senior physician in the city's infirmary,
and I *had* made a difference, hadn't I?

But now?
Now maybe it was time
to become a Bloomsbury doctor!

Uncle Sam

You know how there's always somebody
in a family everybody looks to for guidance?
Ours was my mother's brother Samuel Romilly.

When Father died,
Uncle Samuel rushed to Lausanne
to help mother bring me and Annette back to London.
We took the long way home,
"avoiding any places through which my sister
passed with her husband when she left the country,"
Uncle Samuel explained, fearing the memories
"too painful for her to endure."

Even as a child I saw how my father's death
crushed my mother's spirit.
Any widow in Georgian England faced enormous challenges,
but especially my mother, only twenty-eight.
"Never did any woman adore a husband
with more passionate fondness than she did hers,"
Uncle Samuel lamented, finding a place for us in Paddington.

We moved around a lot,
Chichester and Southampton on the Sussex coast,
Gloucester and Worcester,
but all the way through, Uncle Samuel
was like my surrogate father.

Sir Samuel

While in the eyes of Aunt Anne
I languished among the Mancunians,
Uncle Samuel's career was a meteor in the sky.

Seven kids to raise—
the last one, Frederick, would come in 1810—
he spent a lot of time and energy in law and politics,
hauling in 17,000 pounds a year,
high-profile clients like Maria Anne Fitzherbert,
the Prince of Wales' lover,
raising his own profile among the elite.
The Prince even offered him a seat in Parliament,
but he turned it down.

When the Whigs came to power in 1806,
about a year after I'd completed
my first manuscript of synonyms—
about 15,000 words total, 99 pages, entitled
Collection of English Synonyms Classified and Arranged—
in my King Street apartment in Manchester,
Lord Granville appointed Uncle Samuel solicitor general,
and he entered the House of Commons,
an MP from Queensborough.
That very same year, Uncle Samuel was knighted.

The Suicide

I was his physician as well as his nephew.
Known as "the honestest man in the House of Commons,"
Uncle Samuel was loved by the whole nation.
It seemed his death was all my fault.

Aunt Anne had died from cancer
just three days earlier, at Cowes Castle
on the Isle of Wight, after suffering for weeks,
her pain and distress a blow to her husband;
dying so young, only forty-four.
Insomniac, Uncle Samuel feared he was going mad,
insanity running in the family.

I took it upon myself to break the news
when Anne finally died.
He quickly became unhinged, his whole body
twitching uncontrollably, the spasms like waves
under his skin and over his body.
He moaned that "his brains were burning hot."

But even though he expressed a desire to recuperate
in the country, I insisted he return to Russell Square.
Sitting in the same chaise with his daughter Sophia,
Uncle Samuel tore at his flesh, drawing blood.

Why didn't I see the signs?
I was his doctor! I should have been more attentive!
My medical practice was flourishing, thanks to my uncle.
I'd been elected as a fellow at the Royal Society.

Still a bachelor, closing in on forty,
I also lived in Bloomsbury, just two blocks away.
Amidst all those reminders of his dear wife,
Uncle Samuel asked to be left alone in his room.

Downstairs, we heard a crash.
I ran up to his bedroom, pried open the door.
Uncle Samuel, only wearing a shirt,
staggered next to the washstand, blood everywhere.
He'd slit his throat with a razor.

Gesturing for pen and paper, he scribbled a couple of words
before dropping to the floor, dead.
"My dear . . . I wish . . ."
He'd started a letter to his dear wife Anne.

I had to accept the fact, then,
that I was a failure as a physician;
clinical practice was not for me.
I would devote myself to research, to writing.

Don Samuel

That cur Byron, enraged as a rabid dog,
snarled and fumed when Uncle Samuel
helped his wife, Annabella,
the mathematician, secure her separation
from the depraved brute, in 1816.

They'd separated only two years after the marriage.
Annabella'd discovered her husband's affair with Susan Boyce,
the Drury Lane Theater actress where he was a director,
feared he was going mad,
suspected incest with his half-sister, Augusta Leigh.
Not long after their daughter Ada's birth,
Annabella travelled to her parents' home in Leicestershire,
never saw her husband again.

(Their daughter, Ada, likewise a mathematician, worked
with Michael Faraday, Charles Babbage,
all the great mathematical minds of the day.
Ada wrote the first algorithm
intended to be processed by a machine.)

Only a year after Uncle Samuel's death,
the manky maggot published his spiteful verses
in the first canto of his satirical epic poem *Don Juan:*
"Like the lamented late Sir Samuel Romilly . . .
Whose suicide was almost an anomaly . . .
(The jury brought their verdict in 'Insanity.')"

Such gratuitous nastiness.
I certainly didn't shed a tear
when the bloody bastard died
in Greece five years later.

I'd just met Mary Hobson that year,
the loveliest creature in England,
sixteen years my junior,
soon the mother of our son and daughter.
I couldn't have been happier.

Dylan Thomas's Substitute for Inspiration

The British academic David Holbrook
in *The Code of Night* notes Thomas' preoccupation with words,
disparaging the fixation on his *frozen* metaphor;
he notes the references to *Roget's Thesaurus*
spackling the manuscript of his final poem,
"Poem on His Birthday," to mark his 35th :
"Oh, let me midlife mourn by the shrined
And druid herons' vows"—
middle age, approaching death,
like Dante in *The Inferno,*
halfway to the biblically allotted seventy.

Two hundred pages of revisions at Harvard,
another couple hundred at the University of Texas,
all on this single poem.
An academic's wet dream.

"I like to treat words as a craftsman does his wood
or stone or what-have-you, to hew, carve, mold, coil,"
the poet once explained.

The notes in Thomas' worksheet
refer to 189 in Roget, for "wynd"
("Through the wynds and shells of drowned / Ship towns
to pastures of otters.")
and under tent or covering (223), construction (161),
noting the numbers 223/161/424 (veil), scribbled
to the left of the handwritten draft.
Covering, cover; canopy, tilt, awning, baldachin, tent, marquee.

Oh those herons! "Herons spire and spear."
"Herons, stepple stemmed, bless."
"Herons walk in their shroud."
So like priests! "And wishbones of wild geese."

And so the poem ends:
"As I sail out to die."
Eternal rest. Annihilation. Decease. Demise. Departure.
Mortality. Parting. Passing.
Silence.

Roget's Strumpet

In her diary for February 19, 1956,
seven years and a week
before her suicide,
head in the oven at the age of 30,
Sylvia Plath wrote, "Today my thesaurus,
which I would rather live with
on a desert isle than a bible,
as I have so often boasted,
lay open after I'd written
the draft of a bad, sick poem,
at 545: Deception, 546: Untruth,
547: Dupe, 548: Deceiver."

A week later, Plath would write about
her first kiss with Ted Hughes—
"that big, dark, hunky boy"—
whom she would marry that June,
confessing, "I already have a lover,"
calling herself, "Roget's strumpet."
Flirt, coquette, whore, trollop,
wench, hussy, slut, nymphomaniac:
unchaste woman, easy lay.

The Houdini Séance

"I know the story," I interrupted Jeff, who was trying to enlist me for his Halloween scheme. "A guy named Gordon Whitehead sucker-punched him in the gut in his dressing room at the Princess Theater in Montreal, and he died ten days later in Detroit, on Halloween."

"Yeah, but—"

"And he didn't believe you could actually talk to the dead, anyway, had a big fallout with Sir Arthur Conan Doyle about mediums and spirits and such."

"Yeah, but—"

"His wife Bess kept trying to contact him on Halloween for the next ten years before *she* gave up, too! Tossed in the towel. So what makes you think we're going to talk to Harry Houdini on Halloween? I'd rather go out to a bar in Kenmore Square. The Landsdowne or maybe The Bullpen."

"That's just it, Ben! It was *here,* right here in the Charlesgate, before it became an Emerson College dorm, almost a century ago, when it was all private apartments, before there even *was* a 'Kenmore Square.' It was still called Governor's Square then! Houdini actually attended séances right here, to try to expose that Beacon Hill woman for *The Scientific American.* If we hold a séance *here,* I mean, what are the chances?"

"Not enough to persuade me to change my Halloween plans, Jeff."

"But Madame Griselda! She's the real thing! Warren ran into her in a place on Hanover Street. And what's more in the spirit of the holiday than a séance? Come *on!* It'll be fun! I don't believe in that shit either, but it'll be *fun.*"

In the end, Jeff and Warren twisted my arm and I agreed to attend the Halloween séance in their room that night—candles, incense, everybody holding hands and closing our eyes. The whole nine yards. Besides, with its turrets and towers, the Charlesgate *looked* "haunted," and it was a cold, windy autumn evening, the perfect ambiance.

They'd invited three of our coed classmates, too, Shelley, Brenda and Alison, the three of them as skeptical as we were, but just as game.

"Woo-woo!" Shelley mocked when they arrived, wiggling her fingers, thumbs in her ears. We all laughed. But when the medium arrived, we were all on our best behavior—polite, respectful.

Madame Griselda sure looked the part, lots of makeup, caked all over her cheeks like a clown, gypsy earrings and bright red headscarf, dark, oily Medusa curls. Her accent could have been straight out of the Carpathians—via Hollywood or Hanover Street, anyway.

"Are we really going to speak with Houdini?" I asked, as we all sat down.

"I am not in control," Madame Griselda advised. "I am only a channel for the spirits." Alison rolled her eyes.

We took our seats around the table, a round low-set coffee table Warren had taken from the sidewalk on Beacon Street. Somebody had discarded it from one of the brownstone apartments. Mainly it was used to roll joints and stack textbooks. All that had been cleared for the candles and incense holder, a little Buddha with a plate on his lap where the cones of incense went. The sandalwood fumes were making me want to sneeze. I was twitching my nose to suppress it, when Madame Griselda started to snarl and meow like a cat. We'd all had our eyes closed, of course, to summon the spirits—Madame Griselda had cautioned us to do so—but now I raised a lid and looked at Brenda, whose eyes had become wide as full moons.

"I see a black cat," Madame Griselda announced, and now Brenda rolled *her* eyes. Then she closed them again.

"Who. Who. Who," Madame Griselda chanted, and I wondered if this were supposed to be an owl, if she were summoning her familiar, like something out of *Macbeth,* maybe.

Only, that's when I remembered my family's black cat, Houdini, from when I was a kid. *A black cat!* I'd named him. I'd just learned about Harry Houdini, his famous escape tricks—from straitjackets, handcuffs, jail cells, bound up in boxes sunk beneath the sea, and I'd asked my parents if we couldn't name our cat Houdini. They of course said yes.

Houdini was not allowed to go outside. My mother didn't want him chasing the birds. My father said it wasn't safe and that he might run away. People had it in for black cats, he warned, especially on Halloween. But Houdini used to gaze longingly at the birds and the squirrels outside the living room window, his ears perking up with a hunter's alertness, his tail wagging. It was always a joke in the house, when the front door opened, if one of us was just coming in, and Houdini made a mad dash for the door.

One day when my parents weren't home, I took pity on Houdini and let him out. The predictable happened. He was struck by a car.

I was sobbing when my parents finally got home, though I made up a story how Houdini had escaped while I had the door open and was fetching the mail. How guilty I felt!

Meanwhile, Madame Griselda had started to purr, I swear.

"He say, 'You not responsible,'" she said, looking around at all of us.

"What's that supposed to mean?" Warren asked. "Who's not responsible? For what?"

Madame Griselda shook her head. "He say, 'You not responsible. Not your fault.'"

"Maybe she means Gordon Whitehead," Jeff speculated. "Not responsible for Houdini's death."

"Ah! The spell is broken!" Madame Griselda declared, staring at Jeff, clearly blaming him, and she began to gather her paraphernalia.

"That's it?" Warren cried. He seemed about to argue, until Alison stood up and thanked her profusely, and then Brenda and Shelley chimed in with their thanks, too, and the séance was over.

"You need money for a cab?"

After Madame Griselda had left, we decided to go to a pub. "A black cat!" Jeff exclaimed. "What a ripoff."

But I *knew*.

Karl van Beethoven Considers Suicide

I was ten years old
when my uncle Ludwig became my guardian,
accusing my mother of murder,
denouncing her as a whore,
even though tuberculosis killed my father.

My uncle embarrassed me,
the loud voice brought on by his deafness,
the Viennese calling him crazy,
his long beard giving him the appearance of a vagrant,
once arrested for peering into windows.

The custody battles went on for five years,
first one, then the other bringing suit.
Sure, my mother lived beyond her means,
was once convicted of embezzlement
when I was five years old,
but she loved me.

In the end, I have to admit,
life with my uncle was a lot more comfortable,
even if he made me take piano lessons,
for which I had no talent.

Is it any wonder I attempted suicide
when I was twenty, shooting myself
at the Rauhenstein ruins in Baden?
The bullet only grazed my temple,
but I spent the rest of my life
combing my hair forward to hide the wound.

The Heiligenstadt Testament

I felt like *ein kompletter Trottel*
when my uncle's letter was discovered
after he died. Written to his brothers in 1802,
it's sometimes called a "suicide note,"
spelling out the depths of Ludwig's despair
at losing his hearing, though he'd live
another quarter of a century.

I'd always made jokes behind his back.
Was hast du gesagt? I mocked.
What did you say?
After mimicking him, I'd raise my voice,
repeating my question.

Of course, you can almost hear his arrogance
when he writes about "the *one sense* which ought to be
more perfect in me than others."
He could be so infuriatingly smug.

"With joy I hasten to meet my death,"
he writes his theatrical farewell,
and again I want to kick him,
as if he's the hero of his own *Eroica* Symphony,
Immanuel Kant in his own mind,
dedicated to the categorial imperative,
bitterly remembering the hell he put me through,
taking me from my mother
trying to make a musician out of me,
sending me to school after school—
though yes, he *did* provide me
a better life than Mutter ever could.

"Come when thou wilt,
I shall meet thee bravely."
Oh, please!

Königin der Nacht

I outlived them both,
but that doesn't mean
I feel vindicated or triumphant.

Ludwig dragged my name through the Austrian mud,
calling me "an extremely depraved person,"
adding "Johanna's evil, malevolent and treacherous,"
hinting I'd killed his brother, my husband.
He was always so *superior,*
the sanctimonious Ludwig van Beethoven.
"Never, *never* will you find me dishonourable,"
he declared, and yet,
he drove my son to suicide, didn't he?

Thank goodness Karl failed at *that,* too.
He didn't make Ludwig's life easy, it's true,
after Ludwig stole my son from me,
running away at twelve, fleeing home to his mama;
expelled from school after school;
abusing Ludwig's servants, stealing money.

True, Karl stayed with his uncle
when Ludwig was dying, but why not?
He inherited Ludwig's entire estate!

After a brief military career,
Karl married, failed at business,
but lived comfortably off his inheritances,
tossing me and Ludovika, his illegitimate
half-sister, born out of wedlock
the year I lost Karl in court, the occasional crumbs.
Still, I wept when Karl died,
leaving four daughters and a son of his own.
What mother wouldn't?
But it still angers me he named the boy Ludwig.

Pranayama

> "Life is absolutely dependent on the act of breathing."
> —Yogi Ramacharaka, *Science of Breath*

In a forest clearing
outside the anonymous Belarus village,
miles from Minsk,
the Nazis dug a deep, wide trench
like a castle moat,
heaped the Jews into it,
then covered the living with dirt,
saving their bullets for the front.

The soldiers shot only those
who managed to climb out,
picking them off as they emerged
like pop-up figures in a penny arcade.

Later, the peasants reported the ground
rose and fell, rolled in waves,
like the sea,
for the next three days,
as people tried to dig their way out.
Or maybe they were just breathing.

Bambi

> "What happened, mother? Why did we all run?"
> —Bambi to his mother

His grandchildren glued to the TV,
Shapiro spoke to his son.
"The guy who wrote Bambi?"
he mused, nodding to the screen.
"A Jew. Felix Salten.
Lived in Vienna. Prolific writer.
Plays, short stories, librettos, essays.

"Five years after he wrote *Bambi*,
somebody translated it into English,
and that's when it became a bestseller.
But Salten sold the movie rights in 1933
for a thousand bucks,
and when Disney made the movie in 1942,
he didn't get a dime in royalties.
Not only that,
but the Nazis banned his writings in 1936,
and when they took over Austria
a couple years later,
Salten fled to Switzerland,
where he died in 'forty-five."

Here's where Grandpa lowered his voice.
"Salten also wrote a best-selling porn novel,
Josefine Mulzenbacher." Then, mouthing the words:
"Subtitled, 'The Life Story of a Viennese Whore.'"

Furtive as a pickpocket,
Shapiro's son looked over at his kids;
oblivious, enthralled, they watched
Bambi, in all his innocence,
pursued by the wild dogs.

Escape from Treblinka

It was August, a year after the camp opened,
a death camp where 900,000 Jews were gassed
along with a few thousand Romanis,
set up by the Nazis as part of "Operation Reinhard,"
to increase the rate of genocide
achieved by the *Einsatzgruppen,*
the Germans' mobile shooting squads.
The *Sonderkommandos*—the corpse handlers—
revolted, no longer able to endure the strain,
killing several SS in the process,
but we prisoners were also inspired
by the Warsaw Ghetto Uprising,
seizing weapons from the SS storeroom.
Several hundred of us fled.

Marcus, a priest who used to be a Jew,
ran with me. I'd taken a machine gun
from one of the dead Germans.
It was pandemonium,
everybody trying to get away.

The Germans shot at us,
attempting to prevent the escape,
and Marcus got shot in the leg.
He couldn't move.

"Samuel," he pleaded, "shoot me.
I don't want to go back there."

"Look back at the camp," I told him,
"Look back at Treblinka,
where your wife and child were killed."
Then I shot him in the head.

Jimmy Blanchard Waits for the Light to Change

"Who are we?" the woman with the bullhorn shouts,
a mask over her mouth and nose.

"Strippers!" several dozen women roar back,
waving placards outside City Hall.

"What do we want?"

"Our jobs back!"

Gimme a break!
I don't begrudge anybody making a living,
but this "First Amendment" argument
sounds too much like flag-waving!
Dressing a pig up in lipstick.

Because of the spike in Covid infections,
the mayor banned all indoor and outdoor dining,
capped attendance at gyms, malls and museums,
all indoor recreation establishments—
except strip clubs and hookah bars!
Those he ordered completely closed.
A little too cozy. Between dances,
the girls mingle with guests, after all,
goes with the territory, part of the job.

But then that jackass club-owner, Postlethwaite,
got all self-righteous, threatened a lawsuit.
"We do a deep disinfectant sanitization," he boasted,
the big words puffing him up,
making him feel all smart and responsible.
"The HVAC's exceptional, and the girls? The performers?
Six feet from the poles to the patrons, easy!

This is clearly an attempt
to strip us of our freedom of expression!
No pun intended," he quipped, smirking,
aiming for that late-night show-host wit.
"But Liberty always has its opponents, don't it?"

The light at East Fayette and Holliday changes,
red to green. I honk at the girls as I pass them.
Marianne would kill me
if she ever caught me in a titty bar.

Tina James Raises Her Voice

Joy and Iyana started it,
sent out a flier to organize
the protest at Baltimore City Hall,
about forty of us exotic dancers
there to demand our jobs back.

Other live entertainment had re-opened
after the mayor'd shut everything
because of the coronavirus,
why not adult entertainment, too?

I've been dancing ten years now,
but since Fantasies closed a few months ago,
I've had to go back to my FedEx job
just to make ends meet.
I used to make enough dancing
just two nights a week,
then be home with my kids.
Now? The schedule's just too much
to juggle work and virtual learning.

Some of my friends've turned to websites
where they post nudie sex videos,
interact online with subscribers,
but that's just not me.

So yeah, I drove down from Pennsylvania
to protest outside City Hall,
and when Iyana called out
through that pink megaphone,
"WHO ARE WE?"

I yelled back,
full-throated as MLK's Dream speech,
"STRIPPERS!"

"WHAT DO WE WANT?"

"OUR JOBS BACK!"

Maquiladora Madness

I can't say I actually saw her,
but once I swear
I caught a glimpse
of the Zorro-clad woman, masked,
shrouded in a black cape
as if wrapped with vampire-wings,
lightning-bolt blond hair
a blinding streak behind her,
leap onto the city bus
as it swayed like a pack animal
down the bumpy *calle*.

Sure enough, next day,
I heard about the bus driver
on that same bus,
about an hour later,
found with twin bullet holes
like a forlorn red gaze out of his forehead,
his penis sliced off,
hanging out of his slack-jawed mouth
like an undercooked sausage.

She'd just got so sick of those leering bus drivers,
tobacco, tacos and beer on their breath, bad teeth,
taking advantage of the maquiladoras,
knowing those women depended on them
to get to their night shift in Ciudad Juarez,
raping with impunity, even mutilating,
torturing and dumping their bodies.

The rumors spread thick as unrefined Pemex oil,
so I'm not the only one
who thinks he saw the avenger.

There's even a rumor she left a note
signed "Diana the Huntress,"
but that sounds too literary to me.
This lady was straight out of the comic books,
the bloody vengeance just as final,
the vigilante's do-it-yourself justice
just as sweet.

Andrew Jackson's Parrot

The daily trivia quiz asked
about the vulgar pet parrot
that disrupted the funeral of a president,
with a list of four to choose from—
Jackson, Truman, Roosevelt, Washington;
Andrew Jackson the obvious answer.

The former president buried at The Hermitage,
his Nashville mansion,
Jackson's bird Poll swore like a sailor,
repeating words it had obviously learned
from its owner.
Guests at the somber occasion aghast,
disturbed, horrified; the bird removed.
What had it said?

No record of what it actually said exists, of course,
but I like to think, it squawked,
"You murderous fucking piece of shit!
I hope you rot in hell for the cruelty
of your shitty 'Trail of Tears,'
the suffering you caused,
you motherfucking prick.
I hope every Creek and Seminole
you encounter in the Afterlife
shits and pisses all over
your cocksucking worthless soul.
The 'Indian Removal Act' should be shoved up
your useless asshole every fucking second
throughout eternity,
and I hope it hurts like hell."

The Day Sadat Died

The day Sadat died,
I was halfway across the world
in Watertown, Mass., having rented a room
in a house with two other guys
a couple of blocks away
from a Greek Orthodox church
and Arax, the Armenian market.
Closing in on thirty—not sure
if I was chasing age or age was chasing me—
unemployed, another novel manuscript
just rejected by another publisher,
I felt as beat and alienated
as Lee Harvey Oswald.

LENNON LIVES! somebody's spray-painted
in billboard-sized letters
across a fence on Mount Auburn Street.
I passed it every day on the 71 bus
from Harvard Square to Watertown.
He'd been gunned down in New York
less than a year before.

The following spring, on the same bus
I would read the Boston Herald tabloid headline:
HINCK'S SHRINK STINKS,
the ongoing account about the trial
of Reagan's would-be assassin.

My girlfriend saw Sadat's entourage
pass the café in Cairo
where she and her colleagues—
all studying Arabic abroad
for a year at the American University—
sat drinking tea,

Sadat in the victory parade
commemorating Egypt's crossing of the Suez Canal.
In less than an hour he'd be dead.

Assassin

A few months after Chapman
gunned down John Lennon,
I was in New York
visiting a friend.

We smoked a joint,
walked through Central Park
that cold bright February day,
chatting about whatever
came to mind,
emerging at Seventy-second Street.

My Olympus OM-1
with the telephoto lens
like the barrel of an elephant gun
slung around my neck,
I offered to shoot Roger
in front of the Dakota.

As I fiddled with the focus ring,
a little disoriented by the dope,
a blond woman swept out
from the building,
past the servile doorman,
celebrity self-conscious, glamorous
in big Onassis sunglasses,
cocooned in full-length fur.

Seeing me aim at Roger,
she ducked her head,
threw her hand in front of her face,
as if to deflect a blow,
hailed a passing taxi,
which swerved to the curb
like a sedan in a police thriller.

The cab headed downtown,
a getaway car
blending with the traffic.

The uniformed doorman approached us,
now menacing as a cop on the beat.
Roger and I walked briskly
up Central Park West.
I never did figure out
who that woman was.

Before He Left the Room

I've lived in Baltimore more than half a century,
originally from Trenton.
Came here for college, Johns Hopkins, 1969.
So I was here that night in November, 1971,
when the King played the Civic Center—
now "Royal Farms Arena,"
the way they all cave to corporate sponsorship these days—
but my friends and I disdained him
in favor of The Beatles and the Stones, Dylan,
Jefferson Airplane and The Doors.
No way we'd wait in line to score tickets,
$5 and $10 a pop (scalpers would sell them for as much as $100),
his fans these ancient people in their 30's,
screaming like the teens they'd been in the fifties.
"Help! I need tickets for Elvis!
A matter of life and death!"
somebody pleaded in the newspaper's classifieds.

But six years later, married, working downtown,
Cassady and I thought, why not?
It was May, we'd been married two years;
it was our anniversary.
A friend gave us the tickets:
we didn't even need to stand in line.

But Elvis embarrassed us,
mumbling lyrics like a drug bum, abruptly
leaving the stage for half an hour,
Cass and I—the whole crowd—restless in our seats.
"A call to nature," he apologized when he returned,
muttering something about an ankle twist.

At the end of the performance,
no standing ovation, the reviews next day
mixed, damning with faint praise.

"Almost a caricature of himself," one wrote,
~~as if erasing him from the stage.~~

Less than three months later,
Elvis would be dead,
sprawled across his bathroom floor.

Commencement

"I knew her at Forest Park High,"
Ron, the Jewish guy who ran the drycleaning shop,
told me when I came in for my shirts.
"She was Ellen Cohen then, class of 'fifty-nine.
I remember she was in the co-ed choir."

In another month it'd be the twenty-first century.
I was on my way home from work,
always loved shooting the breeze with Ron.
There'd been a story about Mama Cass Elliot
in the local newspaper, dead a quarter century.

"Just two weeks before she graduated,
she went off to New York to seek her fortune.
She wanted to be an actress.
Her mother worked at Social Security headquarters,
in Woodlawn. Needless to say she disapproved."

Ron rang me up at the register.
I handed him a bill, he gave me change.
I had stuff to do, ready to leave,
but Ron had memories to spill,
a life-long Baltimorean.

"Took her years, but she made it big.
Absolutely *hated* being called 'Mama Cass,'
but that's where she made her mark,
even though her career had its ups and downs
after the Mamas and the Papas broke up.

"Mayor Schaefer always knew an angle when he saw it,
declared August 13, 1973, "Cass Elliot Day,"
had a parade and everything, marching bands,
clowns, politicians, antique cars,
Cass and her mom in a Cadillac limousine.

"They ended up downtown at Hopkins Plaza, Willie Don handing her the Forest Park diploma, fourteen years late, along with a key to city." Ron sighed. "Cass'd be dead less than a year later, heart failure, in her Mayfair apartment, London."

The Scourge

When Friedman died at forty-one
only nine weeks after the AIDS diagnosis,
the horror of the last century
flooded back like Hurricane Harvey,
all those people dropping like leaves
throughout the eighties and early nineties.

The author of the Broadway musical,
Bloody, Bloody Andrew Jackson,
Friedman gathered accolades
like a magnet iron filings.
"One of the most brilliant and promising
people in the American theater,"
Oskar Eustis eulogized.

The artistic director of the Public Theater,
where *Hair* was first performed in 1967,
and *Hamilton* fifty years later,
went on to warn Friedman's death was
"a shot across the bow for anybody
who thinks this disease
is not deadly anymore."

Antarctic Discoveries

We found Captain Robert Falcon Scott's body in the middle of November, lying in a tent alongside Wilson and Bowers, three stiff corpses bundled up like mummies in their sleeping bags, nearly buried in a snowdrift. They'd reached the Antarctic pole back in January, only to find Amundsen, the Norwegian, had already driven his flag into the Pole, claiming the discovery five weeks ahead of him. Captain Scott had always seen Shackleton as his main rival. Such a sad irony in the discovery of his mistake.

But now we found this, the three of them perishing on the Ross Ice Shelf on their return trip, just a few months later. The last entry in Scott's diary, dated to the end of March? It was bitter. He blamed his failure on bad weather and bad luck—not on bad planning.

We set off from Cape Evans the 29th of October, eleven of us, to see if we couldn't discover their whereabouts, certain we wouldn't find them still living. Two weeks later we found their bodies.

We learned from Scott's diary that Edgar Evans had died in February. A month later, Lawrence Oates, who'd been suffering from frostbite, had left his companions in their tent with the words, "I am just going outside and may be some time." He'd had enough. His meaning was plain. That left only Wilson, Bowers and Scott, trapped in their tent by a fierce Antarctic blizzard, only eleven miles from One Ton Depot, their destination.

Scott's final words in the diary, from that previous March, eight months before we discovered them, said, "We shall stick it out to the end, but we are getting weaker."

The snow was higher than the door of their tent when we found it. They were trapped inside. Scott was half in and half out of his sleeping bag. The other two had been resigned to their fate, apparently sleeping to their death. The frost had made Scott's skin yellow and transparent. That's how Tryggve Gran described it in his journal, anyway. To me it was a nightmare, a ghostly paleness, appropriate to the desolation of the ice around us. I'll never forget it as long as I live.

After the burial service, a modest but respectful observance, we collapsed the tent over their bodies. Then we built a snow cairn to mark the graves. What else could we do? Tryggve used his own skis to build the cross above the cairn. He used Scott's own skis for the trek back. He was determined that the skis should complete the journey back, he said, "and they will."

"Jarvis, are you coming?" Lt.-Surgeon Atkinson, the leader of our party, shouted after me when I lingered by the site.

"Turn stored tension into creativity,"

the yoga teacher murmured,
placid as water on a pond.
"Yoga says we are creativity itself."

I always found Jason's vague patter soothing,
the spidery dude who taught our class.
We were doing camel pose, I think.
Or was it cobra pose?
I forget, but with cobra pose,
he usually told us,
"turn venom into nectar."
In baby pose he'd tell us to be
"safely ensconced in the universal womb."

I always left the yoga class
feeling a bit more optimistic,
flexible in my body, for sure,
also a little more meditative,
but his words always made me think
of the squiggly ants
marching across the wall
on the eye doctor's chart,
those lines that got smaller and smaller
as you went down.

"What happens on your yoga mat
is what becomes possible in your own life,"
Jason voice buttered us
as we rolled our mats across the floor.
"Do your best
and be so blessed,
and walk in radiance in this life."

The Sex Nerve

After a series of cat-cows,
followed by downward dogs and cobra pose,
Kevin instructed us to do long deep breathing
while we clutched our ankles,
bent over in butterfly pose.

"It'll help loosen your lower back,
opens your hips,
and works on what the yogis call
the sex nerve," he informed us.

The sex nerve? He made it sound mysterious,
an ancient Vedic rite only for the initiated.
The Land of Lingam and Yoni.

"Interlace your hands under your pinky toes,"
he went on, "Elongate and straighten your spine."
But I was still stuck on "the sex nerve."
What the hell was it?
What did it do?
I thought of the Kama sutra,
those acrobatic sex poses,
the promise of endless orgasms.
I looked over at Melanie, pulling herself down
so her head nestled on her knees.
What exactly was her sex nerve up to now?

But then Kevin had us back on our feet,
arms aimed front and back in a T,
front knee bent in Warrior II,
followed by Triangle pose.

Later I'd look it up,
but all I got was scientific jive
about the pudendal nerve, the pelvic nerves,
the hypogastric nerve (thoracolumbar sympathetic),
components of the autonomic system.

Free Your Hips

"Free up your hips
and make your life less predictable,"
the beatific yoga instructor tells us,
as we move from downward dog
to whatever-you-call-it,
right knee on the floor,
balancing on the left foot,
left leg bent, hands resting
on the left thigh.

When we move next to a bowing pose,
hands pressed to the mat,
feet parallel, about a yard apart,
she cautions us not to grip anywhere.
"Gripping is just a habit," she tells us,
"the way that fear is a habit.
It's been said that fear is excitement
without the breath."

I'm still freeing up my hips,
trying to figure out exactly
what she means by that.

Linger Stink

"Identify with your true identity," our yoga instructor told us, "and walk in radiance in this life." We'd just completed an exercise where we lay on our backs, holding our ankles, and raised our hips up and down. Now we lay flat on our backs in Shavasana—corpse pose.

"Oh, please, Arnie," a voice in the back that belonged to a guy named Blake murmured, "can you just freeze the mystical bullshit? You aren't some sort of swami, for Christ's sake."

A slender bald man, Arnie had lived in Bethesda for maybe half a dozen years now, having come east for college from Keokuk, Iowa, about a decade before. Or so he'd told us when the hatha yoga class began six weeks back.

Nobody said anything. We continued to lie on our backs. Silence shrouded us. It was almost as if nobody had spoken. I opened my eyes and looked at Arnie in front of the class. He was sitting upright on his heels in rock pose, his eyes closed, head bent, meditating. I turned my head in Blake's direction. I thought of Blake as "the chia pet": he had thick hair all over his arms and legs, even on the backs of his hands, and he had a big beard. I think he was a computer programmer or something. Blake was also flat on his back on his mat, along with the other dozen or so students. The room was silent. I heard a clock ticking somewhere. But it felt like somebody had farted and that everybody was pointedly pretending nothing had happened.

I closed my eyes and lay back on my mat. And then, for no reason I could see, the Cranberries' song from about thirty years ago, "Linger," floated into my head. *You know I'm such a fool for you . . . do you have to, do you have to, do you have to let it linger?*

After another thirty seconds, Arnie told us to turn over and turn around, lie on our stomachs and put our hands under our shoulders. Then he told us to stretch up.

"Inhale and raise your upper body, then slowly come back down," he instructed in that dreamy voice he used when he led us through the asanas—the yoga poses. "Cobra pose will help turn venom into nectar."

"Oh fuck you," Blake snarled, getting up and rolling his mat up. He headed for the studio door, opened it and left, closing the door gently behind him.

Again, it was as if nobody had noticed what had just happened. We just continued to raise our upper bodies up and lower them back down while breathing deeply.

Do you have to, do you have to, do you have to let it linger?

Birdwatching

"Video! Video! Video! Video!" A bird sings high up in an ash tree. Gordon catches a flash of red, walking along the Jones Falls Trail. But it wasn't the cardinal's urgent car-alarm call he'd heard. What bird made that noise?

Just ahead, under the bridge, the crazy guy sits around his campfire, his sleeping bag and kit spread around him like a living room without walls, the bridge its ceiling. Except when he bellows at his unseen demons, the crazy guy is harmless. He never tries to intimidate passersby, never asks for food or money, lost in his own world. The Fool on the Hill is Gordon's private name for him. A beard bushy as Walt Whitman's, he makes Gordon think about hidden genius, undiscovered talent. Talent for what? Gordon has seen a ukulele among his possessions, which include a thermos, a plastic carryall, and a battered little grill, but he's never seen him play the instrument. Is it just for show?

"Video! Video! Video! Video!"

Gordon looks around, catching the Fool on the Hill's eye. He's hunkered over his campfire, up on his haunches. Gordon nods, friendly, then looks away.

"A wren."

For a moment Gordon isn't sure if the Fool on the Hill is talking to him or to himself. Just another elusive animal noise, but he turns to look at him.

"Video! Video! Video! Video!"

The Fool on the Hill jerks his head in the direction of the sound.

"Wren," he repeats.

"Thanks!" Gordon moves down the path, feeling the man's eyes on him. He feels like a giant, ungainly bird. He wishes he could sing. He wishes he could fly.

Video! Video! Video! Video!

Wise Man

Depending on which lawyer or financial advisor got to the gym first before going to work, the TV in the men's locker room was tuned either to Fox News or MSNBC—either Morning Joe Scarborough and Mika, or whatever dim-looking blond crossing her legs on the Fox couch next to the grinning white guy sitting beside her. I honestly didn't care which, just there to change into my swimming trunks and go for my morning swim, though I confess I am a Democrat. But it caused arguments that sometimes almost came to blows. Guns, abortion, election integrity, racism, insurrection. Donald Trump.

So thank goodness for Brian! He was the roly-poly homeless dude who made a point of introducing himself to everybody, sticking his mitt in your face while you pulled off your trousers and hung them on a hook. A little annoying, but well-meaning all the same. Sure, the well-to-do gym members, liberal and conservative both, frowned on him, or gave him wary side-eye glances. But really, who wouldn't? He was an anomaly. The guy spent the night on the couch, showered and brushed his teeth before heading over to breakfast at Catholic Charities. Was he a freeloader? Did he pay membership dues? Nobody ever saw him actually working out, though I *did* occasionally see him in the hot tub by the pool.

Because he was there all night, Brian was in charge of the remote—possession being nine-tenths the law, as they say—and he always had the TV tuned to Turner Classics, watching heartwarming old movies with Jimmy Stewart, Maureen O'Hara, Judy Garland and Gene Tierney, *Singin' in the Rain* or *When Harry Met Sally*. Nothing you could fashion a fistfight around.

Gradually, people in the locker room became more civil around each other. DeGrazia, the accounts manager, started asking Grundeman, the defense attorney, about his family. Akchin, the insurance executive, wished Sandman, the Physics professor, a "good weekend" and recommended a play he and his wife had seen. We all talked about the local sports teams with the enthusiasm of playground children. We all laughed at a good joke when Eddie Hall, a noted wisecracker who worked in city government, regaled us with one of his yarns.

But then, one day Brian, always ignored by the rest of us, sitting there like a lump on the couch in front of the TV, never included in the jokes or well-wishes, announced he'd gotten a job helping a friend haul trash, and he was moving into the subsidized-housing high-rise on Roland Avenue. We all shook his hand and wished him well.

And then the Fox News-MSNBC wars resumed.

"DeGrazia," I heard Grundy mutter as I headed down to the pool. "What a fascist."

There she is, your ideal

Only seven when Dad left us,
sneaking away in LA
after him and Mom had traveled from Waco,
I got a job in Buck Hogan's medicine show,
singing, dancing, riding trick ponies, skits,
all through the Depression and into the War,
until Mom took us back to Texas.

Back in Tyler, eighteen years old,
I enrolled in secretary school—
typing, shorthand, filing systems—
when Mister Parker asked me
to represent his bank in the East Texas beauty contest.
I almost said no. Who needs that?

But then one contest led to another
till I won Miss Texas,
hopped a train to Atlantic City.
"Deep in the Heart of Texas" won it for me,
the newspapers calling me "the Texas Tornado."

But Miss America was as much curse as blessing.
I still remember Groucho Marx saying,
"You're almost articulate—for a bathing beauty."
That stubby little runt looked like a rodent.
Who was he to sneer?

I was #MeToo before #MeToo.
I got roles in Hollywood and TV,
but I had to fight off more men than I could count,
dragging me to the casting couch,
as if their reward for the roles I got.

Ed Sullivan, Johnny Carson—
I was on all those shows,
but the high point of my career?
Raising the morale of all those soldiers
when we toured the military bases.

At ninety-seven, I'm just glad
I've lived long enough to see women
fight against inequality and sexual harassment.
I was a feminist before there was a movement.

The Sex Side of Life

Wilkinson, the prosecutor, seemed to relish the words he read aloud to the jury that April afternoon in 1929: "The man's special sex organ or penis, becomes enlarged and stiffened," the words like acid burning his throat, the delicious taste of moral indignation. "It easily enters the passage in the woman's body called the vagina," he went on, the sweat gleaming on his lip. You could tell he was enjoying himself. "By a rhythmic movement of the penis in and out, the sex act reaches an exciting climax or orgasm . . ."

Leaning over the jury box rail, Wilkinson crumpled the blue pamphlet in their faces. "Pure and simple smut," he denounced the sex manual I'd written to educate my children. He warned that the children of our country would be led "not only into the gutter, but below the gutter into the sewer." Oh, there's nothing quite so satisfying as the rush of self-righteousness, is there?

The law I'd broken was the Comstock Act, named for the anti-vice crusader who died about the time I'd written *The Sex Side of Life* for my two young sons. My pamphlet had become so popular, churches, schools, the YMCA requested copies, which I sent through the mail, thus violating the act. I was fined $300.

Of course, we appealed—the ACLU represented me, free of charge—and the next year the U.S. Court of Appeals ruled in my favor, saying the defendant, Mary Ware Dennett, discussed the phenomena of sex in decent language, in a manifestly serious spirit that was not "obscene."

The upshot of the trial? In no small way we paved the way for Joyce three years later when *United States v. One Book Called Ulysses* allowed the novel to be published in the U.S.A. without fear of prosecution.

The Sex Side of Life went on: "This is followed by a sensation of peaceful happiness and sleepy relaxation. It is the very greatest physical pleasure to be had in all human experience."

Even better than moral indignation and Puritanical outrage!

Rivals

Margaret could be such a bitch.
I met her when she spoke about birth control
at a Heterodoxy meeting,
our Greenwich Village suffrage group.
Later, I invited her to lunch, impressed by her talk—
all I'd known about birth control before
(a taboo subject, after all)—
was condoms, pessaries, douches and sponges,
none of them really accessible.

When the feds indicted her
for sending her monthly pamphlet, *The Woman Rebel,*
through the mail—violating the Comstock Act,
for which I'd be tried fifteen years later—
she skipped her court date, fled to Montreal.
She'd spend time in prison for her views.
She walked the walk, said I only talked the talk.

We'd collaborated on the launch
of the *Birth Control Review* in 1915,
but over time we had arguments,
and when Margaret founded The American Birth Control League,
she snubbed me.
Sanger told my friend the Brit feminist Marie Stopes
she "considered Dennett outside the pale of honesty & decency,"
which Marie later relayed to me.

Still, I felt compelled to defend Sanger
after the police raid at Town Hall,
when Margaret was not permitted to speak,
but when I tried to talk to the press,
Margaret's friend, Juliet Barrett Rublee,
shoved me aside, sneering,

"This is *our* affair; we don't want you in it."

See what I mean?

About the Author

Charles Rammelkamp lives in Baltimore, Maryland, where he writes poetry and fiction. Recent works include the poetry collections, *The Field of Happiness, A Magician Among the Spirits,* and *Transcendence.* A chapbook of flash fiction titled *Presto* was also recently published.

Rammelkamp is Prose Editor for Brickhouse Books, the longest continuously publishing literary publisher in Maryland.

www.ingramcontent.com/pod-product-compliance
Lightning Source LLC
Chambersburg PA
CBHW072156160426
43197CB00012B/2405